A Couple of VEGANS in the KITCHEN

DANIELLE REEVES & MASON CHAPMAN

Credits:
Photography: Dimaggio Escobedo of D.E.Lenswork
Make-up: Omar Perez Instagram - beautybyomar

INTRODUCTION

When we decided to put our recipes to paper, it was due to the barrage of messages that we (and you!) receive daily pertaining to food, choices in products, what to eat and when, etc. Knowing the constant bombardment to our psyches regarding our meals, as young adults, we wanted to share what we think would be a beginning place of healing for our bodies. Our thinking is and will be this: If we put a stake in the ground now, establishing healthy and sustainable eating habits, the results will be continued health and self-healing in our future. Some would say we might be too young to influence or show expertise in the culinary food world, and they are right. But most of us do not profess to be the rocket scientist of culinary arts. Most of us are happy with simple recipes that bring health and wholeness to our plates and families. We are writing this book for you. We want the world to be healthy, happy, and whole. Hopefully, this book gets us all a little closer.

Regarding our recipes, we encourage you to change and alter to your liking. We have experimented with all kinds of ingredients and encourage you to do the same. There are many substitutions! Any recipe we have listed for packaged foods, such as pizza dough, you are welcome and encouraged to make from scratch. We do however realize that time restrains us all, so we have listed ingredients that are store-bought for your convenience. The truth of our mission is that compromising on taste with a plant-based menu and lifestyle is not necessary. You and your family can eat tasty meals with little work, but flavor packed to please. There are many brands to try, and we love to buy from local farmers, keeping our local economy in place. So just try. With our book, it should be easy to eat well and pay it forward to your health in 60 minutes or less. Regardless of who is cooking, we hope to be joining you in the kitchen.

OUR STORY

Meet Bruce the pig! Bruce was quite instrumental in changing our lives for the better and forever. Before this little piglet gained 100 lbs. and outgrew his first home, our home in the city, sending him to his new home on our farm in Louisiana. He was a wickedly smart little runt squealing his way to whatever he wanted. When he was ready to eat, a few loud annoying sounds, and presto! Bruce was fed on the spot. But his real strength was not his eating habits but how quickly people, from friends to family, gravitated to him creating bonds which were not forgotten. Bruce was one of the lucky pigs. Bruce lives on the farm versus most pigs like him who are born in a slaughterhouse, kept in a little pen with fifty other pigs, and killed when they reach the desired weight. We started the natural progression of eating the vegan lifestyle without even knowing it, thanks to Bruce. Now, we refuse to tell people how to eat and live their lives, but for the sake of being humane, we have made it OUR mission to help end factory farming because Bruce matters! We hope you find your cause and remember to eat like tomorrow matters too. Bon Appétit!

CONTENTS

OUR FAVORITE INGREDIENTS

Milk
Califia Farms
Ripple

Coffee Creamer
Nut Pods
So Delicious

Butter
Earth Balance
Miyoko's
I Can't Believe It's Not Butter Vegan

Yogurt
Oui Dairy Free, by Yoplait
So Delicious
Silk Almond Milk
Chobani, non-dairy

Cheese
Ricotta – Kite Hill
Parmesan – Follow Your Heart Violife
Mozzarella – Daiya
              Miyoko's
Provolone – Violife
Swiss – Daiya
Cheddar – Daiya, So Delicious

Cream cheese
Tofutti
Daiya

Sour cream
Tofutti
Good Karma

Egg
JUST Egg
Follow Your Heart
Ener-G egg replacer (We use this mostly when baking or for batter when frying.)

Whip cream
So Delicious

Condensed milk
Let's Do Organic

Ice cream
Ben and Jerry's Non-Dairy
So Delicious
Oatly (They have tasty milk as well.)

Acai
Sambazon

Semi-sweet chocolate morsels
Enjoy Life
Simple Truth Organic Semi-sweet Vegan Chocolate Chips

Marshmallows
Dandies

Sugar
Wholesome
Just Panela

Brown sugar
Wholesome
Big Tree Farms

Pie crust
Wholly Wholesome (gluten free and not gluten free available)

Biscuits
Annie's
Immaculate

Crescent rolls
Annie's
Immaculate

Tortillas
Mission
Siete (gluten free)
La Tortilla Factory (gluten free and not gluten free available)

Pasta
Ancient Harvest (gluten free)
Barilla (gluten free and not gluten free available)

Tortellini and Ravioli
Kite Hill

Mayonnaise
Just
Vegenaise
Hellmann's Vegan

Pesto
Seggiano

Tomato sauce
Rao's Homemade Marinara Sauce
365 Organic
Monte Bene

Bouillon cubes
Edward & Sons Not Chick'n Bouillon Cubes

Worcestershire sauce
Annie's
Kroger

Refried beans
Amy's

Bacon bits
McCormick Imitation Bacon Chips
Frontier Co-op

Bacon
Sweet Earth
Lightlife
Morning Star Farms

Ham
Tofurky
Yves

Sausage
Beyond Meat
Morning Star Farms
Dr. Praeger's
Field Roast

Pepperoni
Yves
Good & Green

Meatballs
Gardein

Hot dogs
Lightlife
Field Roast
Tofurky
Beyond Meat (We use this for the waffle corndogs.)

Jackfruit
The Jackfruit Company
Upton's Naturals
Native Forest

Hearts of palm
Private Selection
Native Forest
365 Everyday Value

Fish fry
Zatarain's
Louisiana
Slap Ya Mama Cajun

Shrimp
Sophie's Kitchen
All Vegetarian, Inc.

Tuna
Sophie's Kitchen
Good Catch

Chick'n
Wholesome
Morning Star Farms
Gardein
Beyond Meat
Dr. Praeger's

Ground "beef"
Beyond Meat
Gardein
Pure Farmland
Simple Truth Emerge

Ground "beef patties"
Beyond Meat
Gardein
Pure Farmland
Impossible
Sweet Earth

Philly cheesesteak "meat"
Gardein beefless tips (We used these diced for the Philly cheesesteak.)
Gardein beefless strips (You can use this for the Philly cheesesteak or the street tacos.)

HOW TO BE MORE SUSTAINABLE
Plastic bags – say "No, thank you."

Bring your reusable coffee mug

Bring a reusable water bottle

Metal, bamboo, and paper straws over plastic

Eat local and seasonal

Take shorter showers

Walk or ride a bike if you can

Save paper

Eat plants

KIDS MENU

HOT POCKETS

PREP TIME
20
Minutes

COOK TIME
30
Minutes

SERVINGS
4

1 refrigerated pizza crust

¾ cup shredded cheese

Plant-based pepperoni, sausage, or ham (You could also do veggies.)

1. Preheat oven to pizza crust instructions, usually around 400 degrees.

2. Cut pizza crust into 8-10 rectangles.

3. Place cheese, plant-based protein, or veggies on one half of each rectangle being careful to keep food off the edges.

4. Fold over the empty side of the rectangle, covering the ingredients on each rectangle.

5. Crimp the edges of the pockets closed with a fork.

6. Cook for 20-30 minutes, or until browned on top. Cooking time will vary based on size of hot pocket. Allow to cool for a few minutes and serve.

VEGGIE PINWHEELS

PREP TIME
5
Minutes

COOK TIME
5
Minutes

SERVINGS
8

4 large carrots

1 cup spinach

3 green onions

½ cup cucumbers

8 8-inch tortillas

1 cup hummus or cream cheese, purchased or homemade

1. Peel and shred the carrots and cucumbers.

2. Chop the green onions and spinach into small pieces.

3. Spread about 2 tablespoons of hummus or cream cheese onto a tortilla in a thin layer.

4. Sprinkle a thin layer of vegetables on top, taking care not to overfill and leaving the very top of the tortilla without vegetables.

5. Starting from the bottom of the circle, tightly roll the tortilla. As you roll to the top, the vegetables will naturally move up and distribute evenly through the rollup.

6. Use a serrated knife to cut the roll into 6 or 8 pieces. If desired, spear with toothpicks. Refrigerate until serving.

Tip: You can always warm this up on a skillet or panini press. You can also add a plant-based lunch meat.

TACO LETTUCE BOATS

PREP TIME
10
Minutes

COOK TIME
10
Minutes

SERVINGS
6

1 lb. of Beyond Beef ground beef or chick'n

5 ounce can of black beans or any kind bean, cooked and drained

1½ tablespoons chili powder

1½ teaspoons ground cumin

1½ teaspoons smoked paprika

1 teaspoon onion powder

1 teaspoon garlic powder

1 teaspoon Himalayan salt

½ teaspoon ground black pepper

2 heads of lettuce, peeled into cups

2 medium avocados peeled, pitted and diced

½ cup fresh salsa

1 cup of cheese

1 cup sour cream

1. Heat the large skillet to medium. Add the Beyond Beef ground beef or chick'n.

2. Sauté for 7-8 mins or until desired texture, breaking it up with a wooden spoon as it cooks.

3. Add the beans, chili powder, cumin, smoked paprika, onion powder, garlic powder, Himalayan salt, and black pepper. Stir until fragrant.

4. Add ¼ cup of water and bring to a simmer until thickened. Taste and adjust seasoning, if necessary.

5. Spoon taco meat into lettuce cups and top with diced avocado, fresh salsa, and dollops of sour cream. Serve immediately.

WAFFLE CORNDOGS

PREP TIME
15
Minutes

COOK TIME
10
Minutes

SERVINGS
8

2 packages of Beyond Beef sausage links or Lightlife Smart Dogs, cut lengthwise, then crosswise in half.

1 package (8-½ ounces) corn muffin mix

1 cup shredded cheese

½ cup tomato ketchup

½ cup mustard

1. Spray an 8-inch electric waffle iron with cooking spray. Heat to medium heat.

2. Thread each frank piece onto separate wooden skewer.

3. Place on grid of prepared waffle iron, letting ends of sticks hang over sides of waffle iron. Close lid. Cook franks 2 or 3 mins or until heated through. Remove from waffle iron.

4. Prepare corn muffin batter as directed on package. Stir in cheese.

5. Spread half the batter onto bottom grid of waffle iron. (Batter will not completely cover waffle grid.) Place franks over batter letting ends of sticks hang over sides. Spread remaining batter over franks. Close lid. Cook 4 to 6 mins until waffles are golden.

6. Remove waffles from iron in quarters. Cut each quarter in half. Serve with ketchup and mustard.

HOT-DOGS

PREP TIME
5
Minutes

COOK TIME
5
Minutes

SERVINGS
8

1 package of Beyond Beef meat sausage or Lightlife Smart Dogs

1 package of hotdog buns

½ cup tomato ketchup

½ cup mustard

1. Spray skillet with nonstick spray. Heat skillet to medium heat.

2. Cook hotdogs 4-5 minutes or to desired heat.

3. Remove hotdogs from heat and place each one in a hotdog bun. Top with mustard, ketchup, chili (pg.101), and cheese.

STRAWBERRY BANANA PEANUT BUTTER AND JELLY KABOBS

PREP TIME
5
Minutes

COOK TIME
0
Minutes

SERVINGS
2

4 slices of bread of choice

1-2 tablespoons peanut butter of choice (You can use any nut butter.)

1-2 tablespoons jelly of choice (We used organic strawberry jam.)

2 strawberries sliced in half

1 banana slice

1. Make your peanut butter and jelly sandwich. Cut off crust and cut sandwich into 4 squares or triangles.

2. Place one of your sandwich pieces on a wooden skewer and then add a piece of fruit, alternating until all sandwich slices and fruit are on your skewer. Enjoy!

APPLE PEANUT BUTTER TEETH

PREP TIME
5
Minutes

COOK TIME
0
Minutes

SERVINGS
1

1 apple of your choice

Jar of peanut butter about ¼ to ½ cup for one apple, depending on amount you desire. (You can use any nut butter.)

Mini marshmallows

1. Start by cutting the apple into slices. Then cut them into smaller slices.

2. Now put about a teaspoon or two of nut butter onto each slice.

3. Put a row of mini marshmallows across one apple slice. Then sandwich them firmly together. Press firmly until they stick, and you have your teeth!

FROZEN BANANA YOGURT POPS

PREP TIME
10
Minutes

COOK TIME
0
Minutes

SERVINGS
6

3 bananas peeled and cut cross-wise in half

¾ cup vanilla Oui yogurt or flavor of your choice

Sprinkles or toppings of your choice

Popsicle sticks

1. Halve and peel each banana. Insert a popsicle stick into each banana half.

2. Dip bananas into yogurt, using a spoon to coat each banana evenly. Let excess yogurt drip on plate.

3. Add sprinkles or topping of your choice.

4. Place bananas on a plate covered in wax or parchment paper. Freeze until the yogurt has hardened, about 2 hours. (Allow for more time if you would like the banana to be frozen through.)

BREAKFAST MENU

BACON EGG AND CHEESE BISCUITS

PREP TIME
20
Minutes

COOK TIME
20
Minutes

SERVINGS
9

2 tablespoons butter, melted

2 cups shredded cheddar cheese

1 bottle of Just Egg

1 cup plain coffee creamer

½ teaspoon salt

½ teaspoon dry or regular mustard

½ teaspoon black pepper

¼ teaspoon red pepper flakes

8 precooked biscuits

9 slices of bacon, cooked

1. For the casserole: preheat oven to 350 degrees.

2. Pour melted butter into an 8x8-inch baking dish. Cover bottom of pan with shredded cheese.

3. Whisk together eggs, plain coffee creamer, salt, mustard, black pepper, and red pepper flakes. Pour egg mixture over cheese.

4. Bake for 25-30 mins, until top of casserole puffs up and is golden brown. Cool 15 mins.

5. Cut casserole into 9 squares. Fill each biscuit with a slice of egg casserole and top with bacon. Enjoy.

Tip: You can use any plant-based meat such as sausage.

CHICK'N BISCUITS

PREP TIME
15
Minutes

COOK TIME
20
Minutes

SERVINGS
2

Packaged biscuits (or made from scratch)

Plant-based chick'n substitute (if you don't want to make your own chick'n)

2 blocks extra firm tofu, frozen and thawed

Canola oil or any neutral oil, for frying (You can use air fryer as well.)

Flour mixture

½ cup all-purpose flour (gluten free, optional)

1 tablespoon + 2 teaspoons cornstarch

1 teaspoon Himalayan salt

½ teaspoon smoked paprika

1 teaspoon garlic powder

Flax egg (You can use egg replacer.)
2 tablespoons ground flax seed/ flax seed meal

6 tablespoons water

¼ teaspoon Himalayan salt

Breadcrumb mix
½ cup breadcrumbs (We used Japanese panko breadcrumbs. Gluten free, optional)

1. Prepare the flax egg by mixing the water, flax meal, and salt. Set aside and refrigerate for 10-15 minutes until thick.

2. Freeze the blocks of tofu overnight. We remove the tofu from the container with water that we usually store it in and simply place it on a freezer safe tray after freezing. Thaw the blocks for a few hours at room temperature. Squeeze out the liquid using two flat surfaces. (We use 2 cutting boards.) Ensure that the liquid is expelled well. You can also opt to use a tofu press.

3. Slowly break apart the pieces using a knife or your hands. You can follow the natural breaks of the tofu. There will be small pieces that you can clump together so don't worry. Nothing will go to waste!

4. Roll and coat each piece in the flour mixture. For the smaller pieces, you will need to clump and squeeze them together before and after rolling them in the flour mixture for them to stick.

5. After coating each piece in the flour, add ½ cup breadcrumbs into the leftover flour mixture. Mix well.

6. Dip each piece of tofu into the flax egg mixture. Transfer onto the bread-crumb and flour mixture, and coat well. Repeat this step for the rest of the pieces.

7. Heat a pan with the oil. (We used a cast iron pan and added enough oil to submerge at least half of the pieces in oil.) Once hot, slowly add in the tofu pieces.

8. Fry in medium heat until golden brown and crisp, turning each piece halfway through. Once golden brown, remove from the oil and transfer into a strainer to strain off any excess oil. Turn off heat.

HOMEMADE BISCUITS

1¾ cup flour (gluten free optional)

½ tablespoon baking powder

½ teaspoon baking soda

½ tablespoon sugar

1 pinch Himalayan salt

½ cup + 2 tablespoons very cold butter (Place the butter in the freezer for at least 10-15 minutes.)

PREP TIME: 15 Minutes
COOK TIME: 15 Minutes
SERVINGS: 5

1. Preheat oven to 425 degrees. Line a cookie sheet with parchment paper.

2. In a large bowl, whisk together the flour, baking powder, baking soda, sugar, and salt.

3. Grate the frozen/ very cold butter into the dry ingredients and mix with a fork. Move to a lightly floured flat surface and gently knead to bring the dough together, approximately 10-12 times (do not over knead).

4. Gently flatten the dough with the palm of your hand into a rectangle shape. Fold one end into the middle then fold the other end over the first end (like an envelope). Again, gently flatten the dough with the palm of your hand to about 1 inch thick.

5. Cut out 5 circles with a 2½-inch round cookie cutter. Place biscuits on prepared cookie sheet and bake for approximately 12-15 minutes. Brush with melted butter if desired. Serve warm or at room temperature with the chick'n in the middle. Enjoy!

BISCUITS AND SAUSAGE GRAVY

PREP TIME
10
Minutes

COOK TIME
20
Minutes

SERVINGS
6

1 package of biscuits (recipe to make homemade biscuits on page 33)

1 lb. of Beyond Beef ground meat

3 tablespoons Earth Balance butter

¼ cup all purpose flour (gluten free, optional)

3 cups plant-based milk

1. In a large skillet over medium high heat, cook the Beyond Beef ground meat until slightly brown and crumbly. Add the butter and stir well until melted.

2. Sprinkle Beyond Beef meat with flour. Stir and allow to cook for several minutes until the flour absorbs some of the oil and gets golden brown.

3. Add the milk and stir. Continue stirring occasionally over medium heat until gravy thickens, 5-10 minutes.

4. Pair with your biscuits and enjoy!

CROISSANT BREAKFAST SANDWICH

PREP TIME
10
Minutes

COOK TIME
15
Minutes

SERVINGS
4

4 croissants sliced in half

Just Egg

Plant-based packaged ham

4 slices plant-based American cheese

1. Preheat oven to 350 degrees. Cook Just Egg according to container and to your preferred doneness. Set aside.

2. Slice your croissants in half. Set aside.

3. Place about 4-5 slices of ham on bottom of each croissant. Top with a slice of cheese and top with ¼ of your scrambled eggs.

4. Place other half of croissant on top and wrap with foil.

5. Bake in the oven for 10 mins until cheese is melted, if desired.

Tip: You can use English muffins or bagels for the sandwich. You can also use another breakfast meat – sausage or bacon.

B.Y.O. BREAKFAST (BUILD YOUR OWN)

PREP TIME
5
Minutes

COOK TIME
20
Minutes

SERVINGS
2

4 Beyond Beef sausage links or patties

4 slices bacon

2 slices toast

Earth Balance butter

Just Egg

Choice of fruit

1. Heat a large frying pan over medium heat and brush with oil. Add the sausage to the pan and cook until browned on all sides, about 8 minutes.

2. While the sausages are cooking, add the bacon to the pan. Cook the bacon 3-4 minutes per side until desired texture is reached. (We like our bacon crispy.)

3. When the sausages and bacon are done, transfer to an oven safe dish and cover with foil. Keep warm in the oven while you make the other components.

4. Make sure you have a clean frying pan. Pour in Just Egg and cook according to directions on the package. Once scrambled to your liking, add the egg on the plate with your sausage and bacon.

5. Butter the toast and broil it in the oven, or toast in the toaster.

6. Have a side of fruit and enjoy!

PANCAKES

PREP TIME
5
Minutes

COOK TIME
15
Minutes

SERVINGS
6

½ cup all-purpose flour (gluten free, optional)

1 tablespoon baking powder

¼ teaspoon Himalayan salt

1 cup plant-based milk, unsweetened

2 tablespoons Earth Balance butter, melted

1½ teaspoon vanilla extract

1. In a large bowl, stir together the flour, baking powder, and salt.

2. Stir in the remaining ingredients (milk, butter, and vanilla extract) until just incorporated. Avoid overmixing. There should still be lumps of flour in the batter.

3. Heat a nonstick pan to medium heat. Add a teaspoon or two of butter into the pan if crispy edges are desired.

4. Scoop about ¼ cup of batter into the pan for each pancake.

5. Cook until the top of the pancake starts to bubble and the bottom is golden brown (about 3-4 minutes). Flip! Cook on that side until golden brown (about 1-2 minutes).

Tip: Just add this recipe to your waffle iron for the perfect golden waffles. You can also add in your favorite plant-based protein powder, fruit, nuts, and chocolate. In this recipe, make sure you are using baking powder, not baking soda.

FRENCH TOAST

PREP TIME
5
Minutes

COOK TIME
15
Minutes

SERVINGS
4

8 slices of bread

½ cup Just Egg

1 tablespoon oil of your choice (We used canola.)

3 tablespoons plant-based coffee creamer, plain (can substitute plant-based milk)

1 teaspoon vanilla extract

Pinch of Himalayan salt

1. Make sure bread is sliced, and set it aside.

2. In a deep wide bowl, whisk together Just Egg, coffee creamer, vanilla extract, and salt. Whisk until smooth. Set aside.

3. Preheat a large cooking pan on medium-low. Add a couple tablespoons of canola oil and spread it evenly.

4. Dip each slice of bread, as well as the edges, into the egg mixture. (Just batter as many slices as will fit into the pan. If you must cook in two or more batches, batter bread right before adding it to the pan.)

5. Place battered slices into the pan and let it cook for 3-4 minutes on each side, until golden brown. (Repeat with the remaining slices of bread, if needed.)

6. Serve with your favorite toppings, whip cream, fruit, or chocolate.

HOMEMADE TOASTER STRUDEL

PREP TIME
10
Minutes

COOK TIME
10
Minutes

SERVINGS
8

1 package puff pastry

**1 cup fruit preserves or jelly
(We used strawberry.)**

For the icing

2 tablespoons Earth Balance butter

2 teaspoons plant-based milk

⅔ cup powdered sugar

½ teaspoon vanilla extract

1. Preheat oven to 375 degrees.

2. Roll out the puff pastry sheets into two separate rectangles at least 12 by 18 inches.

3. Place 2 tablespoons of jelly on the puff pastry on small rectangles, 2 by 4 inches, with approximately 2 inches between each rectangle. There should be room for 8.

4. With your finger and a small amount of water, wet the areas between the jelly.

5. Place the other sheet on top and press down to adhere the top sheet to the bottom sheet.

6. Cut the areas between the filling. There should be 8.

7. Bake in the oven for 20-25 minutes or until golden brown.

8. While the pastries are baking, mix all the icing ingredients. Add more plant-based milk as needed to get your desired consistency.

9. When the pastries are finished baking, let cool at least 10 minutes. Add icing on top. Eat immediately.

PIGS IN A BLANKET

PREP TIME
10
Minutes

COOK TIME
15
Minutes

SERVINGS
8-12

1 8-ounce tube crescent rolls

1 package Lightlife hot dogs cut into smaller pieces, or mini sausages

4 teaspoons melted Earth Balance butter

1 teaspoon of Himalayan salt

1. Preheat oven to 375 degrees. On a lightly floured surface, unroll crescent sheets and tear where perforated. Cut each triangle into 3 smaller triangles.

2. Place one hot dog piece or mini sausage on the thick side of each triangle then gently roll to thinner side.

3. Transfer to a medium baking sheet, brush with melted butter, and a sprinkle of Himalayan salt, if desired.

4. Bake until golden, 12 to 15 minutes.

B.Y.O. OMELET (BUILD YOUR OWN)

PREP TIME
5
Minutes

COOK TIME
10
Minutes

SERVINGS
2

1 cup Just Egg

1 cup onion, chopped

½ cup red bell peppers, chopped

½ green bell peppers, chopped

½ cup plant-based deli meat slices, diced

½ cup plant-based cheese of your choice

2 tablespoons Earth Balance butter

½ teaspoon Himalayan salt

Hot sauce (a couple drops of your favorite, optional)

Avocado slices or any other veggies (optional)

1. Add ½ teaspoon butter to a large frying pan and sauté the plant-based deli meat and veggies for a few minutes. Remove from heat.

2. In a bowl, whisk together Just Egg and the Himalayan salt.

3. Heat large frying pan with 1 teaspoon oil and 1 tablespoon butter until hot. Add half of the egg mixture and cook on low/medium heat until the bottom of the Just Egg is cooked.

4. Top with half the veggies, half of the plant-based deli meat, and half the cheese in the first omelet. Fold the empty side of the omelet over the toppings. Close the lid and cook until the cheese melts.

5. Repeat with the second omelet.

6. Top with avocado and your favorite hot sauce. Enjoy!

BREAKFAST BURRITOS

PREP TIME
30
Minutes

COOK TIME
30
Minutes

SERVINGS
6

1 cup potatoes, diced small

1 tablespoon olive oil

1 cup plant-based meat sausage, Beyond Beef ground meat

1 cup Just Egg

1 teaspoon Himalayan salt and black pepper, to taste

6 flour tortillas (corn or gluten free, optional)

1 cup cheddar cheese

2 small Roma tomatoes, diced (optional)

¼ cup chopped fresh cilantro leaves

1. Preheat oven to 400 degrees.

2. Lightly oil a baking sheet or coat with nonstick spray. Spread out diced potatoes evenly. Cook for 10-15 minutes until desired texture, set aside.

3. Preheat olive oil in a large skillet over medium high heat. Add plant-based meat and cook until browned, about 5-8 minutes, making sure to crumble the sausage as it cooks. Reserve the oil in the skillet.

4. Add Just Egg to the skillet and cook 3-5 minutes until done. Add salt and pepper to taste and set aside.

5. Lay out 6 tortillas. Top with potatoes, plant-based meat, eggs, cheese, cilantro, and tomatoes. Fold in opposite sides of each tortilla then roll up, burrito-style. Place seam side down, onto prepared baking sheet. Cover.

6. Place into oven and bake until heated through, about 10-12 minutes.

7. Serve immediately and enjoy!

Tip: To freeze, cover each burrito tightly with plastic wrap or aluminum foil. Freeze up to 1 month. To reheat, bake at 400 degrees for 30 mins or until cooked completely through. This recipe can also be made for lunch. Just leave out the eggs and add any veggies you like.

B.Y.O. OATMEAL
(BUILD YOUR OWN)

PREP TIME
5
Minutes

COOK TIME
5
Minutes

SERVINGS
1

½ cup instant oats

1 teaspoon Earth Balance butter

1 tablespoon brown sugar or any sugar you like (optional)

Cinnamon, chocolate chips, raisins, or other mix-ins

1. Bring 2 ounces water to a boil on the stove top.

2. Put all ingredients in a bowl. Pour the hot water over the ingredients, just covering them barely. Wait 3 minutes.

3. Stir and add more hot water if needed to reach desired consistency. (Cook oats according to package.)

4. Add 1 teaspoon of butter to your oatmeal. Add fruit, stir, and enjoy.

Tip: Store dry oatmeal ingredients in an airtight container or freeze for up to 3 months. We call this my homemade instant oatmeal packets.

STRAWBERRIES AND CREAM OVERNIGHT OATS

PREP TIME
5
Minutes

COOK TIME
5
Minutes

SERVINGS
3

1½ cups oats

1½ cups plant-based milk

¼-½ cup water if mixture is very thick

1 cup strawberry or vanilla plant-based yogurt of your choice

2 tablespoons chia seeds (optional)

¾ cup diced strawberries (fresh or frozen)

1 scoop plant-based protein powder (optional)

1. Mix all ingredients together in a pint-sized mason jar. Preferably, let sit in fridge overnight or for at least two hours. Enjoy!

CHUNKY MONKEY PEANUT BUTTER SMOOTHIE BOWL

PREP TIME
5
Minutes

COOK TIME
5
Minutes

SERVINGS
2

1 cup plant-based milk

½ cup vanilla plant-based yogurt

1 tablespoon agave (add more if needed)

2 tablespoons peanut butter

2 tablespoons cocoa powder mix

2 frozen bananas

Topping Options:

Bananas

Chia seeds

Strawberries

Mango

Berries

Granola (gluten free optional)

1. In a blender, add the milk, yogurt, agave, peanut butter, cocoa powder mix, and bananas. (Be sure to add the soft stuff first and the frozen stuff last to make it easier on your blender.)

2. Blend until smooth, about 2 minutes – give or take – depending on your blender.

3. If you want it thicker, add more bananas or use less milk.

4. Pour into 2 bowls equally.

5. Top with your favorite toppings.

ACAI BOWLS

PREP TIME
10
Minutes

COOK TIME
5
Minutes

SERVINGS
1

1 cup plant-based milk

1 Sambazon acai sorbet

1 tablespoon agave

½ banana

Toppings

Banana, sliced

Strawberries, sliced

Blueberries

Granola

Agave syrup

Peanut butter

Chocolate chips

1. Run acai under warm water and break into chunks.

2. Add all ingredients into blender in the order listed.

3. Add in yogurt until smooth. (You can play with consistency. It should be thicker than a smoothie but thinner than ice cream.)

4. Top with some or all the toppings listed. Enjoy!

APPETIZERS

JALAPEÑO CHEESE CORNBREAD

PREP TIME
10
Minutes

COOK TIME
25
Minutes

SERVINGS
8

⅔ cup plant-based milk

½ cup Earth Balance butter

1 egg (egg replacer)

1 cup shredded plant-based cheese – cheddar, jack, or mix

2 medium jalapeños, diced small

1. Preheat oven to 375 degrees. Spray an 8-inch baking pan with nonstick cooking spray.

2. Whisk together cornbread mix, milk, melted butter, and 1 egg (egg replacer) until moistened.

3. Stir in cheese and jalapeños.

4. Pour mixture into prepared pan. If desired, sprinkle with more cheese.

5. Bake for 25-30 minutes or until a toothpick comes out clean. Let sit 5 minutes before slicing and serving.

Tip: Pairs excellently with a bowl of the Texas chili.

OVEN ROASTED PARMESAN ASPARAGUS

PREP TIME
5
Minutes

COOK TIME
8
Minutes

SERVINGS
4

1 lb. fresh asparagus

1 tablespoon olive oil

1 teaspoon minced garlic

¼ teaspoon Himalayan salt

¼ teaspoon pepper

½ cup parmesan cheese

1. Wash asparagus and cut off woody ends.

2. Grab a baking sheet and place asparagus in a single layer on pan.

3. Mix olive oil, garlic, Himalayan salt, and pepper in a separate bowl then brush mixture over asparagus.

4. Sprinkle fresh parmesan cheese over asparagus.

5. Bake at 425 degrees for 8-10 minutes, depending on preference.

6. Broil top of asparagus and cheese at the end if desired.

FRESH SPRING ROLLS WITH PEANUT SAUCE

PREP TIME
30
Minutes

COOK TIME
10
Minutes

SERVINGS
8

2 ounces rice vermicelli or maifun brown rice noodles

1 teaspoon toasted sesame oil

¼ teaspoon Himalayan salt

1 cup torn butter lettuce

2 medium carrots, peeled and cut into matchsticks or sliced into strips with a julienne peeler

1 cucumber, thinly sliced

¼ cup thinly sliced green onions

¼ cup roughly chopped fresh cilantro

½ cup roughly chopped fresh mint

8 sheets rice paper (spring roll wrappers)

Peanut sauce

⅓ cup creamy peanut butter

2 tablespoons reduced-sodium tamari or soy sauce

2 tablespoons maple syrup

1 tablespoon toasted sesame oil

2 cloves garlic, pressed or minced

2 or 3 tablespoons water, as needed for desired thickness

1. Bring a pot of water to boil and cook the noodles just until al dente, according to package directions. Drain, rinse under cool water, and return them to the pot. Off the heat, toss the noodles with the sesame oil and salt, and set aside.

2. Fill a shallow pan (a pie pan or 9" round cake pan works great) with an inch of water. Fold a lint-free tea towel in half and place it next to the dish. Make sure your prepared fillings are within reach.

3. Combine the green onion, cilantro, and mint in a small bowl, and stir.

4. Place one rice paper in the water and let it rest for about 20 seconds, give or take. Wait until the sheet is pliable but not super floppy. Carefully lay it flat on the towel.

5. Leaving about 1 inch of open rice paper around the edges, cover the lower third of the paper with a few pieces of butter lettuce, followed by a small handful of rice noodles, a few strips of carrot, cucumber, and jalapeño. Sprinkle generously with the herb mix.

6. Fold the lower edge up over the fillings, rolling upward just until the filling is compactly enclosed. Fold over the short sides like you would to make a burrito. Lastly, roll it up. Repeat with the remaining ingredients.

7. *To make the peanut sauce:* In a small bowl, whisk together the peanut butter, soy sauce, maple syrup, sesame oil, and garlic. Whisk in 2 to 3 tablespoons water, as needed to make a super creamy but dippable sauce.

8. Serve the spring rolls with peanut sauce on the side. You can serve them whole or sliced in half on the diagonal with a sharp chef's knife.

Tip: You can add tofu, plant-based shrimp, and plant-based chick'n to these spring rolls.

CREAMY MAC AND CHEESE

PREP TIME
5
Minutes

COOK TIME
20
Minutes

SERVINGS
5

8-12 ounces (2-3 cups) sturdy macaroni noodles (gluten free, optional)

Sauce:

⅓ cup Earth Balance butter

⅓ cup all-purpose flour (gluten free, optional)

2 cups plant-based milk

½ teaspoon ground mustard powder (optional)

½ teaspoon garlic powder

¼ teaspoon cayenne pepper (optional)

2 cups shredded cheddar cheese

Himalayan salt and pepper, to taste

1. Cook the macaroni noodles in a large pot of salted water according to package directions, draining them a minute before the "al dente" cooking time.

2. Heat the milk on the stove top until very hot but not boiling.

3. In a heavy bottomed sauce pot, melt the butter over medium heat. Whisk in the flour and continue to cook, whisking constantly, until the mixture turns a light brown color, about 3-4 minutes. Remove from heat.

4. Slowly start pouring in the milk, whisking constantly. (The mixture will look very thick at first and will thin out as you whisk in the remainder of the milk.)

5. Return the pot to the heat and cook the mixture, whisking continuously, another 3-5 minutes or until thickened. The sauce should coat the back of the spoon. (If you put a little bit on a spoon and run your finger through it, the line from your finger should remain.)

6. Stir in the salt, garlic powder, and ground mustard.

7. Return the remaining sauce to the stove. Over low heat, add the cheeses, stirring to melt. (If you're unable to melt in all the cheese, add a bit more milk, a tablespoon at a time, until the cheese is melted completely.)

8. Stir the sauce into the pasta until your desired level of creaminess is reached. We find we use all the sauce sometimes, and sometimes we have a little leftover. Taste and season with salt and pepper if needed or simply serve hot with a sprinkle of parsley.

SPAGHETTI STUFFED GARLIC BREAD

PREP TIME
25
Minutes

COOK TIME
20
Minutes

SERVINGS
4

16 ounces Italian bread loaf

Earth Balance butter and garlic powder, for bread

1 lb. Beyond Beef ground meat

16-ounce can tomato sauce

6-ounce can tomato paste (optional)

1 medium onion, diced

7 ounces uncooked spaghetti

½ cup parmesan cheese, divided in half

⅔ cup mozzarella cheese, divided in half

1 tablespoon Italian seasoning

1 teaspoon Himalayan salt (optional)

½ teaspoon ground black pepper

½ teaspoon minced garlic

1. Preheat oven to 375 degrees.

2. In a large saucepan, boil spaghetti until al dente. Remove from heat and drain.

3. While pasta is cooking, brown Beyond Beef meat in a large skillet over medium heat. Add onion to browning meat. When brown, drain off any excess fat and return to skillet.

4. Add tomato sauce, pasta, Italian seasoning, garlic, salt, and pepper. Mix well. Simmer for 5-8 minutes.

5. Add cooked pasta. Mix well again and remove from heat.

6. While meat sauce is simmering, cut the Italian bread loaf in half using a bread knife. Carve out the middle of each half of the loaf. Remove bread to create a large hollow in each half. Brush insides of the hollows and sides of the halves with butter. Sprinkle with garlic powder. Toast in oven.

7. When bread is toasted, spoon the prepared spaghetti and meat sauce into the hollow of each half, filling the hollows completely. (You will have spaghetti and meat sauce left over). Top with cheeses, dividing between loaves.

8. Bake at 375 degrees for 15-20 minutes or until cheese is melted and golden. Remove from oven and gently cut with a bread knife to serve.

Tip: If you have spaghetti and meat sauce left over, you can freeze this and have a small spaghetti meal later. Or make a third garlic bread boat using half of another Italian loaf. Yummy!

QUESO

PREP TIME
5
Minutes

COOK TIME
15
Minutes

SERVINGS
8

2 tablespoons Earth Balance butter

2 tablespoons flour (gluten free, optional)

1 cup plant-based milk

1 cup favorite plant-based shredded cheese

½ teaspoon Himalayan salt optional

1. Melt butter in a heavy bottom saucepan.

2. Whisk in flour until fully combined and it makes a paste.

3. Whisk in plant-based milk until smooth.

4. Add shredded cheese and salt.

5. Add additional milk until your queso dip reaches the desired consistency.

ELOTES (CORN IN A CUP)

PREP TIME
10
Minutes

COOK TIME
10
Minutes

SERVINGS
4

4 ears corn, shucked (canned or frozen, optional)

2 tablespoons mayo

2 tablespoons sour cream

4 tablespoons Earth Balance butter, melted

8 tablespoons parmesan cheese

1 lime, juiced

Chili powder and hot sauce, for serving

1. Place corn in large pot of boiling water. Cook for 5-7 minutes or until tender. Remove corn and drain.

2. Cut off kernels and place in a large bowl.

3. Mix the corn with mayo, sour cream, butter, cheese, and lime juice until well combined.

4. Serve with chili powder and hot sauce for toppings.

LIL' SMOKIES

PREP TIME
10
Minutes

COOK TIME
25
Minutes

SERVINGS
8

1 package sausages

½ cup **BBQ sauce**

½ cup **chili sauce**

½ cup **grape jelly**

1. Combine sauces and jelly in a saucepan and whisk to combine.

2. Turn heat on medium and put the lid on the pot. After about 5-8 minutes, once the sauce has heated up a bit, whisk again until smooth.

3. Add sausages. Turn heat down to medium-low, replace lid, and cook for about 30 minutes.

4. Serve and enjoy!

Tip: You can also cook this in the crock-pot. Add all ingredients and cook on medium for 1-2 hours.

TEXAS CHILI

PREP TIME
15
Minutes

COOK TIME
50
Minutes

SERVINGS
8

2 tablespoons vegetable oil (can use Earth Balance butter as well)

2 yellow onions, diced

3 garlic cloves, finely minced

2 pounds Beyond Beef ground meat

1 teaspoon Himalayan salt

¼ cup ancho chili powder

2 tablespoons cumin

1 tablespoon paprika

1 tablespoon brown sugar

29 ounces diced tomatoes

1 cup cooked beans (optional, we use black beans)

6 ounces tomato paste

4 cups vegetable broth

½ cup sour cream

2 jalapeños

½ cup shredded cheddar cheese

1. Add vegetable oil, or butter, and onions to a large saucepan on medium-high heat and cook until the onions are translucent, about 6-8 minutes.

2. Add the garlic and cook for 1-minute, stirring well.

3. Add the Beyond Beef ground meat, breaking apart as you cook it for 6-8 minutes, but leave the chunks a bit larger and allow it to sear well.

4. Add in Himalayan salt, ancho chile powder, cumin, paprika, and brown sugar. Stir well cooking for 1 minute.

5. Add in the diced tomatoes, beans (optional), and tomato paste. Whisk well until the tomato paste is well mixed in.

6. Add in the vegetable broth and bring to a simmer. Reduce the heat to medium low and cook for 30 minutes, stirring every fifteen minutes.

7. Add toppings: sour cream, cheese, jalapeños.

SOUPS

POTATO SOUP

PREP TIME
30
Minutes

COOK TIME
20
Minutes

SERVINGS
6

3 tablespoons butter

1 medium onion

3 large garlic cloves, minced

⅓ cup all-purpose flour (gluten free, optional)

2½ lbs gold potatoes peeled and diced into pieces no larger than 1"

4 cups vegetable broth (add in one chick'n bouillon cube, optional)

2 cups almond milk (any plant-based milk works fine)

⅔ cup plain coffee creamer (replaces heavy cream)

1½ teaspoon Himalayan salt

1 teaspoon ground pepper

⅔ cup sour cream

Shredded cheddar cheese, chives, and vegan bacon bits

1. Place soup pot on medium heat. Add garlic and cook until fragrant (about 30 seconds).

2. Sprinkle flour over the ingredients in the pot and stir until smooth (use whisk if needed).

3. Add diced potatoes to the pot along with vegetable broth, milk, coffee creamer, salt, and pepper. Stir well.

4. Bring to a boil and cook until potatoes are tender when pierced with a fork (about 10 minutes).

5. Reduce heat to simmer and remove approx. half of the soup to a blender (Be careful. It will be hot!) and puree until smooth. (Half is about 5 cups of soup, but just eyeballing the amount would be fine. Blender optional.)

6. Return pureed soup to the pot and add sour cream, chives, and cheddar cheese. Enjoy!

BROCCOLI CHEESE SOUP

PREP TIME
10
Minutes

COOK TIME
20
Minutes

SERVINGS
4

1 cup finely chopped onions

½ tablespoon minced garlic

1 tablespoon Earth Balance butter

32 ozs vegetable broth (4 cups)

1 cup matchstick (julienned) carrots

⅓ teaspoon ground nutmeg

½ teaspoon Himalayan salt

6 cups shredded cheddar cheese

32 ounces Nutpods coffee creamer (substitute any plant-based milk)

1. Sauté onion, garlic, Himalayan salt, and butter until onion is translucent.

2. Add vegetable broth and nutmeg, and bring to a simmer.

3. Add broccoli and carrots, and cook until tender.

4. Add cheese in small amounts, stirring constantly until all is incorporated.

5. Pour coffee creamer in and stir on medium/low until all ingredients are incorporated and soup is heated through. Do not boil.

MISO SOUP

PREP TIME
5
Minutes

COOK TIME
10
Minutes

SERVINGS
4

4 cups vegetable stock

2 tablespoons dried wakame

5 fresh shiitake mushrooms (sliced thinly)

3 tablespoons white miso paste

10 ounces tofu (cubed)

½ cup spring onions (chopped)

1. Add vegetable stock to a pot on the stove and bring to a simmer.

2. Add dried wakame and sliced shiitake mushrooms to the pot.

3. Let the wakame and mushrooms cook in the vegetable stock for around 5 minutes until the mushrooms are cooked. Switch off the heat.

4. Mix hot water to thin the miso paste.

5. Add the miso paste to the pot. Stir it in gently.

6. Add cubed tofu and chopped spring onions, and mix in. Serve immediately.

CHICK'N NOODLE SOUP

PREP TIME
15
Minutes

COOK TIME
45
Minutes

SERVINGS
8

1 package plant-based chick'n (shredded)

2 cups carrots, peeled and chopped

1 medium yellow onion, diced

3 stalks celery, chopped

3-4 cloves garlic, minced

3 tablespoons extra virgin olive oil

½ teaspoon dried thyme

6 cups veggie broth

2 chick'n bouillon cubes

1 cup water

Himalayan salt and freshly ground pepper to taste

2 cups uncooked wide noodles

3 tablespoons fresh parsley, chopped

1. In at least a 6-quart pot, add in shredded chick'n, carrots, onion, celery, garlic, olive oil, and thyme.

2. Next add in vegetable broth, 2 bouillon cubes, water, and season with salt and pepper to taste. (We used ½ teaspoon salt and ¼ teaspoon pepper.)

3. Cover and cook on medium for 45 minutes or until carrots are tender.

4. Now add in noodles and parsley.

5. Cover and cook just until noodles are tender, 5-10 minutes.

TOMATO SOUP

PREP TIME
20
Minutes

COOK TIME
60
Minutes

SERVINGS
8

3 lbs tomatoes. Use ripe, in-season tomatoes or replace with whole canned tomatoes

2 tablespoon balsamic vinegar

2 tablespoon olive oil

1 tablespoon sugar

1 teaspoon Himalayan salt

2 red onions, finely chopped

2 garlic cloves, finely chopped

½ cup basil leaves

2 teaspoons tomato paste

8 cups vegetable broth

½ cup plain coffee creamer

Salt and pepper to taste

Fresh basil leaves to serve

1. Preheat the oven to 400°.

2. Place the tomatoes (if using canned tomatoes, add all the juices as well) in a roasting tray and add the balsamic vinegar, olive oil, sugar, and salt. Stir to combine and place in the oven for 25-30 minutes until the tomatoes are broken down and have started to caramelize.

3. In a large pot, sauté the onions in some olive oil until they are translucent and fragrant. Add the garlic and basil and fry for another minute.

4. Add the roasted tomatoes and more sugar if needed. Stir to combine all the ingredients and pour in the vegetable stock.

5. Lower the heat and cover the pot. Allow to simmer for 10 minutes.

6. Remove the pot from the heat and blend the soup.

7. Add the coffee creamer, and season to taste.

8. Serve the tomato soup with a swirl of coffee creamer and fresh basil leaves with a grilled cheese sandwich. Yum!

REFRESHMENTS

CLASSIC STRAWBERRY BANANA SHAKE

PREP TIME
5
Minutes

COOK TIME
5
Minutes

SERVINGS
1

1 cup strawberries

1 banana

½ cup plant-based milk or coffee creamer

2 scoops plant-based protein (optional)

1. Blend all ingredients until smooth, adding a touch more milk as needed to reach a consistency to your liking. Enjoy!

Tip: For best results, make sure at least one of your fruits is frozen before blending. This will make your smoothie thick and frosty!

SPINACH PINEAPPLE BANANA SMOOTHIE

PREP TIME
5
Minutes

COOK TIME
5
Minutes

SERVINGS
1

Whole banana

Fresh pineapple, 3 medium-sized chunks

1 cup spinach

2 cups coconut milk (substitute your favorite plant-based milk)

1. Blend banana, pineapple, and one cup coconut milk. Use pulse method about 10-30 seconds.

2. Blend spinach with one cup coconut milk.

3. Combine blended spinach with previously blended pineapple and banana. Enjoy!

Tip: You can replace the milk with water or juice. (We like to use pineapple juice.)

FRESHLY SQUEEZED ORANGE JUICE

PREP TIME
10
Minutes

COOK TIME
10
Minutes

SERVINGS
1

10 oranges

1. Wash the oranges to remove any potential pesticide residue.

2. If the oranges are very firm, roll them on the countertop with your palm while applying downward pressure. This helps break up the individual segments and juice-filled vesicles, releasing more juice.

3. Cut the oranges in half with a sharp knife or peel all the way depending what type of juicer you're using.

4. Using a handheld citrus reamer, or an electric juicer, twist the flesh of the oranges on the reamer to extract the juice and pulp.

5. Pour the freshly squeezed orange juice into a glass and enjoy!

FRESHLY SQUEEZED CELERY JUICE

PREP TIME
5
Minutes

COOK TIME
5
Minutes

SERVINGS
2

10 celery stalks

1. After you have washed them, put celery stalks through the power juicer.

2. Allow the juice to chill in the fridge for a few minutes if you wish. (We usually leave it in there while we clean the juicer).

3. Drink within 8 hours.

Tip: Use all organic produce if possible. This will make your skin glow.

LEMON GINGER
TURMERIC DETOX DRINK

PREP TIME
5
Minutes

COOK TIME
20
Minutes

SERVINGS
6

6 cups water

1 chunk ginger (5-6" in length)

3 cinnamon sticks

1 teaspoon ground turmeric

½ teaspoon cayenne pepper

½ fresh lemon

1. Peel the ginger and dice into thin slices.

2. In a large pot or saucepan, combine the peeled and sliced ginger and water over high heat. Bring to a boil then turn to low heat and let simmer for approximately 10 minutes.

3. After 10 minutes, add the cinnamon sticks, turmeric, and cayenne, and simmer on low heat for another 10 minutes, stirring occasionally.

4. Remove from heat, let cool and strain.

5. This makes about 6 cups of a concentrated version of the detox tea which you can store in a glass container in the fridge. You can drink this concentrate warm or cold and add fresh lemon juice to taste right before you enjoy.

6. We personally like to add ¼ cup of this mixture to ½ tablespoon fresh lemon juice and 6 ounces hot water.

HOT CHOCOLATE

PREP TIME
1
Minutes

COOK TIME
5
Minutes

SERVINGS
4

4 cups plant-based milk

¼ cup unsweetened cocoa powder

¼ cup granulated sugar

½ cup semisweet chocolate chips

¼ teaspoon pure vanilla extract

1. Place milk, cocoa powder, and sugar in a small saucepan. Heat over medium-low heat, whisking frequently, until warm (but not boiling).

2. Add chocolate chips and whisk constantly until the chocolate chips melt and distribute evenly into the milk.

3. Whisk vanilla extract, serve immediately for hot chocolate.

Tip: For frozen hot chocolate put in freezer for 30-45 minutes until desired consistency.

DINNER

CHICK'N FETTUCCINE ALFREDO

PREP TIME
10
Minutes

COOK TIME
20
Minutes

SERVINGS
4

16 ounces fettuccine noodles (gluten free, optional)

1 package of plant-based chick'n or our homemade chick'n recipe on page 33

Alfredo Sauce

2 tablespoons Earth Balance butter

2 garlic cloves

1 tablespoon all-purpose flour (gluten free, optional)

2 cups coffee creamer original flavor

¼ cup sour cream

1 cup grated parmesan cheese

Himalayan salt and fresh cracked black pepper to taste

1. Cook fettuccine according to the package instructions. Make sure not to overcook the noodles so they are not too mushy. Drain and set aside.

2. Prepare your chick'n and slice it in small chucks according to your liking.

3. Alfredo sauce: measure all ingredients before starting to cook.

4. In a medium, heavy bottom sauce pot, melt butter over medium heat. Once butter is melted, add pressed garlic. Cook garlic until it's fragrant, and then sprinkle flour over it. Stir until flour is all mixed with butter. Then slowly pour in coffee creamer while constantly stirring.

5. Gently stir the mixture together and let it heat through. (Don't let it boil!) Once coffee creamer is hot, whisk in sour cream, parmesan cheese, salt, and pepper. Lower heat to medium-low and gently stir until grated cheese melts.

6. Keep cooking over medium-low heat for about 5 minutes, stirring often.

7. Once sauce is ready, mix it with cooked pasta and sliced chick'n. You can top it off with some fresh parsley and more grated parmesan cheese.

Tip: You can also turn this into Shrimp Alfredo. Our favorite brand is ALL VEGETARIAN, INC. We purchase this at an online grocery store called Lucky Mouth Grocery.

CHICK'N POT PIE

PREP TIME
10
Minutes

COOK TIME
35
Minutes

SERVINGS
8

1 lb. of plant-based chick'n cut into 1" chunks

2 large carrots, sliced

2 stalks of celery, sliced

1 small white onion, minced (optional)

1 small bag of frozen peas

2 tablespoons Earth Balance butter

¼ cup of water

1 tablespoon of oil of your choice (for pan frying the chick'n chunks)

⅓ cup of flour (gluten free, optional)

Himalayan salt and pepper to taste

2½ cups of vegetable broth

⅔ cup plant-based milk of your choice

2 pie crusts (We used store-bought.)

1. In a small skillet, heat oil and then pan fry the chick'n chunks. After the chicken is warmed up, set it aside.

2. Heat oven to 425 degrees and line a large pie plate with one pie crust. Prick holes in the bottom using a fork.

3. Meanwhile, chop your veggies, and then add them to a stock pot with ¼ cup of water (frozen peas will add more liquid), and butter. Let the veggies cook while stirring constantly for about 5 minutes over medium-high heat.

4. After veggies are fork tender, add your flour mixture, and coat all your veggies. Then, whisk in the milk first and then broth.

5. Add chick'n, and black pepper. Stir until thick and uniformly creamy.

6. Once mixture is ready, add it to the pie, and then cover the top of the pie with the remaining pie crust. Crimp edges. Be sure to add holes and slits to allow the pie to vent.

7. Bake for 35 minutes or until the pie is a golden-brown color.

8. This pie will not slice nicely if too hot. We suggest allowing the pie to rest for 15-30 minutes, but the slices will still be slightly messy.

Tip: You can make your own pie crust from scratch to add your own personal touch to this recipe.

BUFFALO CHICK'N SANDWICH

PREP TIME
10
Minutes

COOK TIME
10
Minutes

SERVINGS
2

2 tablespoons of your favorite hot sauce

2 pieces of plant-based chick'n or homemade chick'n recipe page 33

4 buns or bread of your choice

1 tablespoon vegan mayo

Lettuce

Avocado

Pickles

1. Prepare your chick'n according to instructions on bag or make our homemade chick'n recipe.

2. Assemble your chick'n sandwich by spreading the mayo on buns. Top with chick'n and garnish with your favorite toppings. Enjoy!

Tip: Our other favorite sauces to have on our chick'n sandwich are agave mustard or BBQ sauce.

CHICK'N AND DUMPLINGS

PREP TIME
15
Minutes

COOK TIME
20
Minutes

SERVINGS
4

¼ cup Earth Balance butter

1 yellow onion, diced

¼ cup all-purpose flour (gluten free, optional)

10.5 ounces of vegetable broth

1 not-chick'n cube

1 cup frozen peas

1 cup frozen sliced carrots

4 cups coffee creamer (plain)

2 cups plant-based chicken, cooked, shredded

1 teaspoon Himalayan salt

1 teaspoon pepper

1 teaspoon onion powder

12 ounces refrigerated biscuits

1. In a large saucepan over medium-high heat, cook butter and diced onions until onions are translucent.

2. Add the flour to the pot and stir well.

3. Continue cooking until the flour just starts to turn golden-brown.

4. Add the vegetable broth and 1 not-chick'n cube to the pot and stir well.

5. Add the coffee creamer and stir again.

6. Bring the liquid to a boil. While waiting for the liquid to come to a boil, cut the refrigerated biscuits into quarters.

7. Once the liquid is boiling, add the peas, carrots, shredded chick'n, salt, pepper, and onion powder to the pot. Stir well.

8. Add the pieces of biscuit dough to the pot and stir gently.

9. Cover the pot and reduce heat to medium low.

10. Continue cooking the chick'n and dumplings for 20 minutes while covered, stir gently every 5 minutes to make sure nothing sticks to the bottom of the pot.

11. After twenty minutes stir well and serve. Enjoy!

Tip: When we have coffee creamer listed for a recipe, keep in mind you can always substitute this with a plant-based milk of your choice.

SLOPPY JOES

PREP TIME
5
Minutes

COOK TIME
15
Minutes

SERVINGS
6

1 lb. Beyond Beef ground meat

½ teaspoon Himalayan salt

2 tablespoons brown sugar

½ tablespoon chili powder

1 teaspoon mustard

1 small onion, finely chopped

½ cup ketchup

2 tablespoons Worcestershire sauce

8 ounces tomato sauce

4 hamburger buns

1. Heat a large skillet over medium-high heat. Add Beyond Beef ground meat and onion, cooking and crumbling the Beyond Beef meat for about 7-8 minutes.

2. Add all remaining ingredients. Stir until combined and let simmer 10 minutes or until slightly thickened.

3. Serve on toasted hamburger buns with a slice of plant-based cheese. Pair with potato chips and a pickle on the side. Enjoy!

BACON GUACAMOLE GRILLED CHEESE

PREP TIME
5
Minutes

COOK TIME
12
Minutes

SERVINGS
1

3 slices of bacon

2 slices sourdough bread

1 tablespoon Earth Balance butter, room temperature

1 slice American cheese

1 slice cheddar cheese

2 tablespoons guacamole, room temperature

1 tablespoon tortilla chips, crumbled (optional)

1. Cook the bacon until crispy and set aside.

2. Butter one side of each slice of bread, place one slice of cheese onto the unbuttered side of one slice of bread followed by the guacamole, bacon, tortilla chips, the remaining cheese and finally top with the remaining slice of bread with the buttered side up.

3. Grill over medium heat until golden-brown and the cheese has melted, about 2-3 minutes per side.

SHRIMP PO-BOY WITH A CREAMY CAJUN SAUCE

PREP TIME
10
Minutes

COOK TIME
5
Minutes

SERVINGS
4

For the Creamy Cajun Sauce:

1 cup mayo

⅔ cup ketchup

1 tablespoon lemon juice

½ to 1 tablespoon Creole seasoning (depending on how spicy you like it)

½ teaspoon garlic powder

½ teaspoon paprika

For the shrimp:

4 tablespoons Earth Balance butter

2 cloves garlic, minced

1 lb. plant-based shrimp, uncooked

Creole seasoning to taste

1 loaf of French bread, cut into 4 pieces

Shredded lettuce, to taste

1. Combine sauce ingredients in a mixing bowl until smooth. Set aside.

2. Heat a large skillet to medium heat, add butter and garlic. When butter is hot and melted, add shrimp.

3. Sprinkle Creole seasoning over the shrimp. It can be a little spicy so only sprinkle to your personal taste.

4. When shrimp is cooked to your desired crispiness, remove from heat. Do not overcook.

5. Split French bread open and divide shrimp evenly between each slice. Top with the creamy Cajun sauce and shredded lettuce, to taste. Enjoy!

Tip: You can add many toppings to this including tomatoes, pickles, and jalapeños just to list a few.

SHRIMP COCKTAIL

PREP TIME
17
Minutes

COOK TIME
5
Minutes

SERVINGS
4

1 lb. plant-based shrimp, cut into small pieces

1 cup ripe tomatoes, chopped

2 tablespoons jalapeños, seeded and finely chopped

½ cup red onion finely chopped

2 cups tomato juice

½ cup ketchup

¼ cup freshly squeezed lime juice

2 tablespoons cilantro and more for serving, chopped

1 large ripe avocado, chopped

Hot sauce to taste

How to cook the plant-based shrimp

1. Bring a pot of water to a boil. Once water starts boiling, add shrimp and cook for about 2-3 minutes. Transfer shrimp to a plate to cool.

2. Reserve 5-7 shrimp for garnish by placing them on a plate. Cover them and place them inside the fridge until ready for use.

3. Chop all shrimp into tiny bite-sized pieces.

How to make shrimp cocktail

1. In a mixing bowl, whisk until everything is combined – tomato juice, ketchup, lime juice, cilantro, and hot sauce to taste.

2. Into this bowl, add cooked shrimp, tomatoes, jalapeño, and red onion. Gently mix until ingredients are well combined.

3. Cover and chill inside the fridge for about 1-3 hours before serving. Right before serving, stir in 1 chopped avocado. Serve inside clear glass. Garnish with reserved cooked shrimp and cilantro. Enjoy!

Tip: Thaw frozen raw shrimp in cold water or by placing the bag in the fridge overnight.

CRAWFISH QUESO BURRITO

PREP TIME
20
Minutes

COOK TIME
25
Minutes

SERVINGS
6

For the crawfish

1 jar of hearts of palm, diced

1 cup of seasoned fish fry (follow instructions on the back of bag)

½ cup oil of your choice

For the queso

1 cup plant-based cheese of your choice

1 cup plant-based milk of your choice

Himalayan salt to taste

For the burrito

6 flour tortillas (gluten free, optional)

1 cup lettuce shredded

1 cup tomatoes diced

1 cup avocado diced (optional)

½ cup jalapeños diced (optional)

For the crawfish

1. Dice hearts of palm no bigger than 1" pieces. Prepare the fish fry according to instructions.

2. Heat a large frying pan on medium heat. Add the oil to the pan, and let it heat up for 3 minutes. Meanwhile, dip the hearts of palm in your prepared fish fry mix.

3. Add your fish fry coated hearts of palm to the frying pan and let them cook 2-3 minutes until they are golden brown. Line a plate with a paper towel and place your cooked hearts of palm on the plate. Cover and set aside.

For the queso

1. In a saucepan on medium heat, add the milk and the cheese.

2. Whisk together until all cheese is melted evenly. Add additional milk if needed to reach your desired consistency.

3. Salt to taste and keep on low heat so it doesn't dry out until you need it.

For the burrito

1. Preheat oven to 350 degrees. Spray 9x13-inch baking dish with cooking spray and set aside.

2. To prepare 1 burrito, spread ¼ of the crawfish, and then add a generous amount of queso down the middle of the burrito.

3. Add your lettuce, tomatoes, and jalapeños, making sure to save enough toppings for the other burritos.

4. Fold in opposite sides of each tortilla then roll up burrito style. Place, seam-sides down, in prepared dish. Repeat with remaining ingredients to prepare 6 burritos.

5. Cover and bake for 20 minutes (until heated through). If you're baking the burritos from the refrigerator while they're still cold, it will take about 30 minutes for them to heat up.

Tip: To freeze in individual servings, wrap each burrito in aluminum foil before baking. Then just remove one (or more) burritos from the freezer when you're ready to eat. To bake individual foil-wrapped burritos straight from the freezer (while still frozen): Place foil-wrapped burrito on a baking sheet and bake at 350 degrees for 45-50 minutes.

B.L.T. SANDWICH (BACON, LETTUCE, AND TOMATO)

PREP TIME
10
Minutes

COOK TIME
10
Minutes

SERVINGS
2

8 slices bacon

½ cup romaine lettuce

1 beefsteak tomato

4 slices sandwich bread

3 tablespoons mayo

½ tablespoon Earth Balance butter

Himalayan salt and pepper to taste

1. Fry bacon in a pan until crispy on both sides, approx. 4 minutes each side. Remove from heat and cool on plate. Wipe the pan clean.

2. Spread butter on each side of the bread slices. In the same pan, toast the bread on each side until golden brown. Cut tomato into thick slices and season with salt and pepper.

3. Swipe a generous amount of mayo on each bread slice. Add lettuce, two slices seasoned tomato, and half the bacon. Top with another bread slice and cut crosswise into two triangular halves. Enjoy!

PHILLY CHEESESTEAK

PREP TIME
15
Minutes

COOK TIME
15
Minutes

SERVINGS
4

1 lb. beefless tips, trimmed and thinly sliced

½ teaspoon Himalayan salt, or to taste

½ teaspoon black pepper, or to taste

1 sweet onion (large) diced

8 slices provolone cheese

4 hoagie rolls sliced ¾ through

2 tablespoon butter, softened

1 garlic clove, pressed

2-4 tablespoon mayo, or to taste

1. Slice hoagie rolls ¾ of the way through with a serrated knife. Dice onions and thinly slice beefless tips.

2. In a small bowl, stir together 2 tablespoon softened butter with 1 pressed garlic clove. Spread garlic butter onto the cut sides of 4 hoagie rolls. Toast the buns on a large skillet or griddle, on medium heat until golden brown then set aside.

3. Add 1 tablespoon oil to your pan. Sauté diced onions until caramelized then transfer to a bowl.

4. Increase to high heat and add 1 tablespoon oil. Spread the super thinly sliced beefless tips in an even layer. Let brown for a couple of minutes undisturbed then flip and season with ½ teaspoon salt and ½ teaspoon black pepper. Sauté until beefless tips are fully cooked through then stir in the caramelized onions.

5. Divide into 4 even portions and top each with 2 slices of cheese and turn off the heat so the cheese will melt without overcooking the meat.

6. Spread a thin layer of mayo on the toasted side of each roll. Working with one portion at a time, place a toasted bun over each portion and use a spatula to scrape the cheesy beefless tips into your bun as you flip it over. Serve warm. Enjoy!

CHEESEBURGER–
Our Favorite Is Our Big Mac

PREP TIME
10
Minutes

COOK TIME
10
Minutes

SERVINGS
5

4 plant-based burger patties

4 burger buns

4 slices of plant-based cheese

Lettuce, chopped or whole

Onion, chopped or cut in rings

Tomato, sliced

Mayo

Mustard

Ketchup

1. Heat large frying pan on medium heat. Place plant-based burgers on frying pan, and let them cook for approx. 4 minutes on each side or until cooked to your liking. Place cheese on top when your burger has one more minute left to cook. Place cheeseburgers on a plate. Cover and set aside.

2. Lightly toast buns in toaster oven.

3. Assemble cheeseburgers. Place plant-based meat patty with melted cheese between the burger buns, and add lettuce, tomato, onion, condiments of your choice. Enjoy!

PIZZA

PREP TIME
45
Minutes

COOK TIME
60
Minutes

SERVINGS
8

1 tablespoon olive oil plus more for brushing

1 lb. fresh pizza dough, store-bought or homemade

½ cup pizza sauce

1 cup plant-based shredded mozzarella cheese

15 small plant-based pepperoni slices

½ cup thinly sliced bell pepper red and green

¼ cup thinly sliced red onions

½ cup sliced white mushrooms

¼ cup sliced olives

½ teaspoon Italian seasonings

Black pepper to taste

Tips: You can add plant-based sausage to this pizza for extra flavor!

1. If using store-bought pizza dough, allow to sit at room temperature for 30 to 45 minutes.

2. Place oven rack in the center position and preheat oven to 475 degrees.

3. Place a 12-inch cast iron skillet in the oven to heat. (any type of pan will work)

4. Lightly flour a work surface, the dough, and rolling pin. Roll the dough out into a 12-inch circle.

5. Carefully remove the skillet from the oven and place on a heat-safe surface.

6. Add olive oil to the skillet and use a paper towel to evenly spread into the pan.

7. Carefully add the pizza dough to the skillet, spreading the edges into the corners of the pan.

8. Lightly brush olive oil on the edges of the crust.

9. Bake the pizza dough for 3 minutes to par-bake the crust.

10. Remove the pizza dough from the oven and evenly spread the pizza sauce over dough.

11. Sprinkle the cheese over the sauce.

12. Add the pepperoni, bell pepper, red onions, mushrooms, and olives on top.

13. Sprinkle the Italian seasonings and black pepper on top.

14. Bake the pizza until the bottom is golden brown and crispy, 10 to 12 minutes.

15. Slice the pizza and enjoy hot.

Tip: We like pizza for breakfast. You can make this a breakfast pizza by just adding plant-based sausage and scrambled Just Egg.

HOMEMADE CHALUPAS

PREP TIME
10
Minutes

COOK TIME
30
Minutes

SERVINGS
4

2¼ cup flour (gluten free, optional)

1 tablespoon baking powder

½ teaspoon Himalayan salt

1 ounce shortening

1 cup plant-based milk

Canola oil, for frying (You can use any oil you like.)

1 lb. Beyond Beef ground meat, cooked

Plant-based cheddar cheese

Lettuce

Diced tomatoes

Plant-based sour cream

Taco sauce

1. Heat the oil in a heavy-duty, shallow skillet such as a cast iron skillet.

2. In a large mixing bowl, add the flour, baking powder, salt, and shortening. Use a fork to mix the ingredients together. Pour the milk into the dry ingredients. Use a wooden spoon to mix ingredients in with the milk to form a ball of dough.

3. Turn dough onto a floured surface and roll until smooth. Mold the dough into a loaf about 8" long. Divide the dough in half, then into fourths. Roll each individual section into a ball and roll out the small ball of dough into a round circle about 4-5 inches wide.

4. Use tongs and carefully dip half of the chalupa dough into the hot oil. Once that half of the dough has begun to fry up but not quite brown, flip the chalupa bread with the other half of the dough frying in the oil. If it doesn't matter to you, just fry on both sides for 2 minutes until golden brown and remove from oil onto cooling rack or plate lined with paper towels.

5. Fill your chalupas with Beyond Beef ground meat, lettuce, cheese, tomatoes, and a dollop of sour cream. Top with taco sauce if desired.

ENCHILADAS

PREP TIME
20
Minutes

COOK TIME
25
Minutes

SERVINGS
6

1 lb. Beyond Beef ground meat

1 small white onion, diced

1 clove garlic, minced

2 tablespoons taco seasoning

½ teaspoon cumin

¼ cup water

8-10 corn or flour tortillas

28-ounces can red enchilada chile sauce

2-3 cups freshly shredded plant-based cheddar cheese

1 green onion, thinly sliced

Plant-based sour cream

Pico de gallo

Salsa/hot sauce

Diced avocado

Fresh cilantro

1. In a large skillet over medium heat, cook Beyond Beef ground meat with diced onions and garlic, breaking up the Beyond Beef meat with a spoon as it cooks. Cook about 8 minutes.

2. Sprinkle taco seasoning and cumin over the Beyond Beef meat and stir in ¼ cup of water. Continue to cook, stirring often, until water is absorbed.

3. Preheat oven to 350 degrees. Pour ½ cup of enchilada sauce in the bottom of a 13"x9" baking dish and spread evenly.

4. Heat remaining sauce in a small skillet, just until bubbly, and then remove from heat. Dip a tortilla in the enchilada sauce to coat both sides then lay flat on a cutting board or plate. Add a small amount of the meat mixture (about 3 tablespoons) down the center of the tortilla, then top with about 1-2 tablespoons of shredded cheese. Roll up both sides and place seam side down in the prepared baking dish. Repeat with remaining tortillas and Beyond Beef meat.

5. Pour remaining sauce over the enchiladas evenly and top with remaining shredded cheese. Feel free to add more or less cheese based on your preferences. Sprinkle sliced green onion on top.

6. Bake uncovered for 20-30 minutes, or until cheese is melted and sauce is bubbly. Let sit 5 minutes before serving. Garnish as desired with optional toppings like sour cream, Pico de Gallo, avocado, sliced green onions, or cilantro. Enjoy!

Tip: You can also make a bean and cheese, or veggie enchilada. Just replace the Beyond Beef ground meat with your favorite beans or veggies or both!

PATTY MELT

PREP TIME
10
Minutes

COOK TIME
30
Minutes

SERVINGS
4

2 large sweet onions, peeled, halved, and thinly sliced

8 tablespoons butter, divided

⅓ cup mayo

2 tablespoons ketchup

½ teaspoon yellow mustard

¼ teaspoon garlic powder

¼ teaspoon ground black pepper

4 Beyond Beef meat burgers

8 slices thick cut sourdough or rye bread

4 slices plant-based cheddar cheese

4 slices plant-based Swiss cheese

1. In a large skillet, melt 2 tablespoons of butter over medium-low heat. Add the onions and cook over low heat, stirring occasionally, until they are golden and soft, about 30 minutes.

2. Make the sauce by combining the mayo, ketchup, mustard, garlic powder, and black pepper. Set aside.

3. Heat a large cast iron skillet over medium-high heat. Add two tablespoons of butter then cook the beyond meat burger patties according to the package instructions. Wipe the skillet clean.

4. Assemble each sandwich by spreading the sauce on one side of all 8 slices of bread. Divide the onions between 4 slices of bread. Top each with a burger patty, one slice of each cheese, and then another slice of bread.

5. Add 2 tablespoons of butter to a skillet over medium-low heat. Swirl to coat the pan with the melted butter. Add the assembled sandwiches and cook until the bread is golden brown. Flip the sandwiches and add the remaining 2 tablespoons of butter. Move the sandwiches around to coat them in butter. Cook until golden brown. Serve immediately.

CHILI RELLENOS

PREP TIME
15
Minutes

COOK TIME
20
Minutes

SERVINGS
6

To make chili rellenos sauce

⅓ cup corn oil

1 medium onion, peeled and quartered

4 garlic cloves

⅓ cup flour

6 Roma tomatoes

1 seeded and stemmed jalapeño pepper

5 cups water

2 tablespoons Himalayan salt

1½ teaspoons Mexican oregano, crushed between your fingers

¼ teaspoon finely ground black pepper

1 bay leaf

1 pinch ground cinnamon

1 pinch ground cloves

Chiles

6 large poblano chiles, fresh

Brine

4 cups water

4 teaspoons Himalayan salt

⅓ cup white vinegar

Cheese

6 ounces plant-based cheddar cheese

Chile relleno batter

2 cups canola oil, for frying

2 eggs (egg replacer)

1-2 cups plant-based milk, depending on consistency (You want it like pancake mix.)

½ cup flour (gluten free optional)

¾ teaspoon Himalayan salt

Garnish

Plant-based sour cream

Fresh cilantro

To make the sauce

1. Heat ⅓ cup corn oil in a medium saucepan over medium-low heat.
2. Finely chop the onion and garlic in a food processor.
3. Sauté the onion and garlic mixture in corn oil until translucent, golden, and almost caramelized. This will take at least 10 minutes.
4. Mix the ⅓ cup flour into the onions and garlic and stir, cooking until flour is lightly browned.
5. Place the Roma tomatoes in a food processor and puree. You should have about 1½ cups pureed tomatoes.
6. Add the jalapeño pepper and onion/garlic/flour mixture from saucepan into the food processor with the tomatoes. Make sure to submerge the onion and garlic roux into the puree.
7. Process everything until all the ingredients are finely pureed.
8. Add oregano, ¼ teaspoon finely ground black pepper, 1 large bay leaf, 1 pinch ground cinnamon, and 1 pinch ground cloves.
9. Bring mixture to a boil while whisking.
10. Reduce heat to medium low and simmer for about 45 minutes, or until you have a nice thick sauce. Cover the saucepan slightly, vented so steam can escape and whisk the sauce occasionally.
11. You can keep the sauce warm over lowest heat, whisking as needed to refresh consistency until served, or reheat and stir before serving.

Peppers

1. Keep the pepper stems intact and place on a grill or under broiler, cooking on each side until evenly blistered and slightly blackened.
2. Immediately place the peppers into a large plastic bag and allow to steam for about three minutes.
3. Carefully slide the skin off each pepper and discard.
4. Cut a slit lengthwise down the side of each pepper. (You need it just big enough to slip a stick of cheese in.)
5. Carefully cup each pepper with one hand and gently run water into the slit to flush out the seeds.
6. Combine 4 cups water, 4 teaspoons salt, and ⅓ cup white vinegar, and soak the chiles in this brine for a few minutes.
7. Cut your cheese into 6 long thin sticks.
8. Remove chiles from brine and blot dry with paper towels.
9. Stuff each chile with one cheese stick by slipping into the pepper slit. Don't panic if you tear a chile. Flour and the batter will seal it up.

Chile relleno batter

1. Pour 2 cups oil into an electric wok and set heat control to 265°F. If you're confident in the kitchen, feel free to use a heavy-duty skillet on the stove with a thermometer to monitor your temperature.
2. Measure ½ cup flour into a sifter or fine mesh colander and dust each of the chiles well with flour on all sides. For torn chiles, apply some extra flour at the seam then slightly overlap the tear.
3. Beat milk, egg placer, and a pinch of salt with an electric mixer.
4. Use a rubber spatula and "frost" a stuffed and floured chile.
5. Hold chile by the stem and place carefully into the hot oil. Repeat with additional chiles, frying only 2 or 3 at a time.
6. Fry the chiles until golden on all sides, turning once with a skimmer or coated tongs until done. It takes about 5 minutes to fry completely.

To serve

1. Drain the peppers between paper towels. If not serving immediately, you can reheat them individually in a microwave or on broil in the oven for 15-20 seconds.
2. Make a pool of warm sauce on the plate and add a chile. Top with a dollop of sour cream and a sprinkling of fresh chopped cilantro.

FRIED AVOCADO TACOS

PREP TIME
20
Minutes

COOK TIME
15
Minutes

SERVINGS
20

To make tacos

Oil for frying

3-4 large avocados, cut into 1"-2" slices

Pack of small "street style" corn tortillas (any type of corn will work)

1 cup panko breadcrumbs (gluten free, optional)

1 cup tempura batter

¾ cup ice cold water

Himalayan salt, and pepper to taste

1 teaspoon red pepper flakes

Cilantro-Lime Crema

½ cup plant-based mayo

½ cup plant-based sour cream

2-3 tablespoons warm water

¾ cup loosely packed cilantro

1 teaspoon cayenne pepper

1 whole lime, juiced

Himalayan Salt and Pepper to taste

Crema

1. Mix all ingredients in a blender until creamy in texture.

2. Set aside.

Tacos

1. Heat oil in a shallow frying pan on medium heat.

2. In a bowl, combine ice cold water, red pepper flakes, and tempura batter. Mix until you reach a pancake-like consistency. Set aside.

3. In a separate bowl, add panko breadcrumbs and season with about 1 teaspoon of salt.

4. Dip avocado slices in tempura batter, shaking off excess liquid.

5. Dip in panko breadcrumbs and set aside.

6. Once all avocado slices are coated, fry on medium to medium-high heat for about 8-10 minutes, turning halfway through.

7. Heat tortillas in the microwave or on your stovetop.

8. Assemble tacos with crema, corn, and other toppings, if desired. (We add lettuce.)

STREET TACOS

PREP TIME
5
Minutes

COOK TIME
20
Minutes

SERVINGS
8

2 tablespoons of vegetable oil

3 lbs. plant-based carne asada meat (Nunos Tacos and Vegmex Grill)

1 white onion, chopped

2 fresh limes, plus extra for toppings

1 bundle of cilantro

Himalayan salt, to taste

Pepper, to taste

½ stick of butter

Mini corn or flour tortillas

1. If using a plant-based meat from Nunos Tacos and Vegmex Grill, you will only need to heat it up in a skillet on medium heat for 10 minutes if frozen and only 5 minutes if not.

2. Squeeze the juice of two fresh limes over the meat.

3. Continue cooking until the meat is heated through.

4. While the meat is heating, melt the butter in another skillet or electric skillet.

5. Fry the mini corn tortillas in the melted butter for 1 minute until they are soft.

6. Allow them to cool slightly.

7. You will need 2 mini corn tortillas per taco.

8. Spoon the meat mixture on the tortilla.

9. Top with cilantro and fresh onions, and serve with limes.

Tip: We purchase the best plant-based meat for tacos, nachos, Tortas, tamales, and really any dish you can think of, or just eat it plain by itself! We order in bulk at Nuno's Tacos and Vegmex Grill, located at 8024 Spring Valley Rd., Suite 8024, Dallas, Texas 75240

CALZONES (PLANT-BASED PEPPERONI AND CHEESE)

PREP TIME
20
Minutes

COOK TIME
15
Minutes

SERVINGS
4

1 lb. pizza dough (gluten free, optional)

½ cup pizza sauce

½ cup yellow onion, diced (optional)

½ cup green bell pepper, diced (optional)

½ cup sliced pepperoni

1 cup mozzarella cheese shredded

1 tablespoon olive oil

1. Preheat oven to 425 degrees. Line a large sheet pan with parchment paper.

2. Divide pizza dough into 4 equal parts, and roll each dough ball into a ¼ inch thick circle.

3. On half of each dough circle, add equal parts sauce, yellow onion, green bell pepper, and sliced pepperoni. Make sure to leave a little room around the edges so you can crimp the calzone shut.

4. Sprinkle the toppings with equal parts shredded cheese. Then fold the other half of the dough over the toppings and crimp the edges.

5. Cut 2-3 air vents into the top of the calzone and place it onto the prepared baking sheet.

6. Brush with olive oil and bake for about 15 minutes or until the dough is fully cooked and the calzone is golden brown.

7. Serve with warmed pizza sauce for dipping.

Tip: You can also make a veggie or plant-based ham and cheese calzone. You can use homemade or store-bought pizza dough. Check your local pizza places (or Italian market) for fresh homemade dough, and store some extra in the freezer. Ensure plant-based meats are cooked and any watery veggies (like mushrooms or pineapple) are cooked and/or well drained.

TORTELLINI WITH TOMATO SAUCE AND GARLIC TOAST

PREP TIME
10
Minutes

COOK TIME
20
Minutes

SERVINGS
4

9 ounces cheese tortellini

2 tablespoons olive oil, divided

½ cup onion, diced

4 cloves garlic, minced

½ teaspoon dried oregano

⅓ cup water

¼ cup vegetable broth

14-ounces jar tomato sauce

1 teaspoon sugar

4 slices of toast

4 teaspoons butter

Plant-based parmesan cheese

Basil and parsley for garnish (optional)

1. Cook onion in 1 tablespoon olive oil until tender. Add garlic, basil, and oregano, and stir until fragrant.

2. Add tomato sauce, water, broth, and sugar and use a spoon to slightly stir.

3. Bring to a boil, and reduce heat to simmer. Allow sauce to simmer and thicken while cooking the tortellini, about 10 minutes. Stir in remaining olive oil.

4. Cook tortellini al dente according to package directions. Drain but do not rinse.

5. Meanwhile, toast bread slices and butter them. After toasted, slice in half and serve with meal.

6. Gently mix cooked tortellini with prepared tomato sauce. Top with parmesan cheese and fresh parsley or basil and serve.

Tip: This recipe makes four one-cup servings. If serving as a main dish, we would suggest doubling the recipe for 4 people.

STUFFED BELL PEPPERS

PREP TIME
30
Minutes

COOK TIME
30
Minutes

SERVINGS
6

1 lb. Beyond Beef ground meat

4 mushrooms, chopped (optional)

¼ cup tomatoes, diced

3 ears of fresh corn kernels or 1½ cups frozen corn

2 stalks of celery, chopped thinly

1 medium onion, chopped

2 cloves garlic, minced

2 14.5-ounces jars tomato sauce

2 tablespoons basil

1 tablespoon oregano

½ teaspoon red pepper flakes

Himalayan salt, and freshly ground black pepper, to taste

1½ cups cooked long grain rice (We use Spanish rice.)

¼ cup chopped Italian parsley

6 bell peppers

1 cup shredded plant-based cheddar cheese or plant-based Monterey jack cheese

1. Preheat the oven to 350 degrees.

2. Brown the Beyond Beef ground meat in a large fry pan over medium high heat for 5 minutes or until cooked almost through. Add the mushrooms, corn kernels, chopped celery, onion, and garlic, and cook until vegetables are softened.

3. Stir in the diced tomatoes, tomato sauce, basil, oregano, and red pepper flakes. Season with salt and ground pepper to taste and cook for 15-20 minutes. Stir in cooked rice and chopped parsley, and cook for another 5 minutes or until the rice is warmed through.

4. Meanwhile, cut off the tops of the peppers and spoon out the ribs and seeds, then rinse. Lightly sprinkle the inside of the peppers with salt and place in a microwave safe dish with ¼ cup water. Cover with plastic wrap and microwave for 5 minutes or until they start to soften.

5. Transfer to a 3-quart baking dish and fill the peppers with the hot Beyond Beef meat and rice mixture. Sprinkle the top with cheese and bake for 20 minutes or until peppers are tender and cheese is browned. Serve hot.

WINGS

PREP TIME
10
Minutes

COOK TIME
18
Minutes

SERVINGS
6

2 cups whole oyster mushrooms

1 cup unbleached all-purpose flour, divided (gluten free, optional)

2 teaspoons Himalayan salt

2 teaspoons onion powder

1 teaspoon dried basil

¼ teaspoon cayenne pepper

¾ cup unsweetened plant-based milk

½ cup corn flakes or corn chips

¼ cup grapeseed oil

1. Place two separate bowls on the counter.

2. In one bowl, put ¾ cup of the flour along with half of the Himalayan salt, onion powder, dried basil, and cayenne pepper. Add all the unsweetened milk, and mix thoroughly to combine.

3. In the other bowl, add the crushed cornflakes along with the remaining ¼ cup of flour and dry seasonings. This bowl will be designated as the "dry" ingredients bowl.

4. Set both bowls aside.

5. Heat a large frying pan on medium-high heat. When the pan is hot, add the oil. Make sure the bottom of the pan is fully covered with oil.

6. Next, separate the mushrooms into smaller pieces so that they are a little smaller than chick'n wings.

7. Dip the mushroom into the wet bowl first and then into the dry bowl.

8. Gently place each batter-dipped mushroom into the hot pan.

9. Let the mushroom fry for about 30 seconds to 1 minute, and then flip it over to fry on the other side. You may repeat flipping to cook evenly on both sides.

10. If using an air fryer, dip the mushrooms into the dry bowl only and place them into the air fryer. Lightly spray with grapeseed oil. Cook at 400 degrees for 18 minutes.

11. Remove the fried mushroom pieces to a paper towel when golden brown on both sides. Serve warm and sprinkle with buffalo sauce.

Tip: You can also use this same recipe to make cauliflower wings. You can use any flavor sauce on the wings including bbq sauce, honey mustard, lemon pepper, and teriyaki.

SUPREME NACHOS

PREP TIME
15
Minutes

COOK TIME
10
Minutes

SERVINGS
6

1 lb. Beyond Beef ground meat

13 ounces tortilla chips

1 package plant-based cheese

3 tomatoes, cubed

2 large avocados, cubed

Green onion, chopped

8 ounces beans of your choice
(optional) We used refried beans.

1-2 teaspoon taco seasoning

Black olives

1. Preheat the oven to 400. Place avocados, tomatoes, and onion in a bowl, set aside. Place Beyond Beef ground meat in the skillet. Season with taco seasoning and sauté on medium heat until meat is cooked through, about 5-8 minutes.

2. Grab another pan and cook beans on medium heat, cook until it starts heating through. Set aside.

3. Put tortilla chips on a baking sheet and add shredded cheese or queso page 73 Place it in the oven for a few minutes to warm up the chips and cheese a bit more.

4. Once everything is heated through and cooked, garnish your nachos. First, sprinkle Beyond Beef ground meat all over the tortilla chips. Add beans, and add tomato salsa. Serve while hot. Enjoy!

QUESADILLAS

PREP TIME
2
Minutes

COOK TIME
6
Minutes

SERVINGS
6

6 fresh tortillas (gluten free, optional)

1 bag plant-based cheese, shredded

1 tablespoon Earth Balance butter

1. Heat a skillet over medium heat and cook each tortilla on both sides until just slightly warm.

2. Remove the tortillas from the pan. Add cheese to half of each and fold in half.

3. Add a little butter to the pan and fry the quesadilla on each side, repeating with each tortilla.

Tip: You can add spinach, mushrooms, bell peppers, Beyond Beef meat, and chick'n. Just to name a few!

HOMEMADE HAMBURGER HELPER

PREP TIME
5
Minutes

COOK TIME
20
Minutes

SERVINGS
6

1 lb. Beyond Beef ground meat

1 small onion, finely chopped

1 teaspoon paprika

1 teaspoon dried parsley

1 teaspoon garlic powder

A pinch to ½ teaspoon cayenne powder

Himalayan salt and pepper, to taste

1½ cups plant-based milk

1½ cups vegetable broth

2 cups elbow macaroni, uncooked (gluten free, optional)

8 ounces tomato sauce

2 cups plant-based cheddar cheese

1. Heat a large skillet over medium heat. Brown the Beyond Beef ground meat, onion, paprika, parsley, garlic powder, cayenne powder, salt, and pepper.

2. Stir in the milk, broth, macaroni, and tomato sauce. Bring to a boil. Cover and reduce heat to a simmer. Cook for 10-12 minutes or until pasta is tender. Stir occasionally to prevent sticking.

3. Stir in cheddar cheese until melted.

LASAGNA

PREP TIME
15
Minutes

COOK TIME
1 hr 30
Minutes

SERVINGS
8

1 lb. Beyond Beef ground meat

1 tablespoon each: oregano, basil, rosemary (or 3 tablespoons of an Italian blend of herbs)

½ yellow onion, chopped

4 garlic cloves, chopped, divided

9 lasagna noodles, boiled al dente

2 jars of your favorite marinara sauce (roughly 48 ounces)

1 16 ounces container plant-based ricotta

4 tablespoon pesto

½ cup plant-based parmesan, shredded

4-5 cups plant-based mozzarella, shredded

1. About an hour before cooking, spread out ricotta on a plate and place a couple paper towels over it to soak up some of the moisture.

2. Preheat oven to 375.

3. Prepare lasagna noodles according to package directions.

4. In a skillet, crumble and cook Beyond Beef ground meat, onion, herbs, and 2 diced garlic cloves.

5. While Beyond Beef ground meat is cooking, add 2 cans of marinara sauce to a large saucepan and warm up.

6. After Beyond Beef ground meat is cooked through, add to marinara sauce. Do not drain.

7. Simmer until you are ready to assemble lasagna.

8. In a bowl, mix ricotta, pesto, 2 diced garlic cloves, and parmesan cheese.

9. Now it's time to layer your lasagna!

10. In a 9"x13" pan, spread a thin layer of sauce.

11. Next, lay out your first layer of noodles and cover with meat sauce.

12. Add a generous layer of mozzarella.

13. Add another layer of noodles topped with the ricotta blend.

14. Sprinkle with more mozzarella.

15. One more layer of noodles and add the rest of the sauce ... and don't put the last cheese layer on yet! You heard me! You are going to cook the lasagna without the epic top cheese layer first!! Cover it with foil, cut a few vents, and bake for 30 minutes.

16. Take the pan out and remove the foil.

17. Now put on that epic last layer of mozzarella cheese! (We like to add a little garlic salt and parmesan to the top for extra flavor.)

18. Bake for another 20-30 minutes until cheese is browned and bubbly.

MEATBALL SUB

PREP TIME
5
Minutes

COOK TIME
10
Minutes

SERVINGS
4

4 sub rolls

16 precooked plant-based meatballs

1 cup marinara sauce (more as needed)

2 tablespoons Earth Balance butter (softened)

½ teaspoon garlic salt

¾ cup shredded plant-based

mozzarella cheese (or plant-based provolone cheese)

1. Preheat the oven to 425 degrees.

2. Combine the meatballs and marinara sauce in a small pan and heat over medium heat.

3. Split the sub rolls in half and then place onto a baking sheet. Spread lightly with butter and sprinkle garlic salt on top. Bake for 3 minutes or until lightly toasted.

4. Place 4 meatballs on top of each sub, then sprinkle with mozzarella cheese. Fold the top over and bake another 3-5 minutes, or until the cheese is melted.

5. Enjoy while hot!

Tip: Marinate your meatballs in your favorite marinara sauce over night after you have cooked them. This allows the meatballs to soak in the sauce and makes them incredibly juicy.

DESSERTS

WENDY'S FROSTY

PREP TIME
5
Minutes

COOK TIME
5
Minutes

SERVINGS
2

½ gallon plant-based chocolate milk

1 can sweetened condensed coconut milk

1 So Delicious whipped cream

1. Mix all ingredients together well by hand and freeze for 45 minutes or until desired consistency is reached. Mixture does not get hard, more like a thick milkshake.

HEALTHY CAKE BATTER BALLS

PREP TIME
5
Minutes

COOK TIME
5
Minutes

SERVINGS
8

½ cup cashew butter, unsalted or nut butter of your choice

2 tablespoons maple syrup

½ teaspoon almond extract

⅓ cup oat flour

1 scoop plant-based protein powder, optional

⅛ teaspoon Himalayan salt

Sprinkles or chocolate chips for rolling

1. In a bowl, mix cashew butter, maple syrup, and almond extract.

2. Add in oat flour, protein powder, and salt. Mix until combined.

3. Place dough in the freezer for 30 minutes to firm up.

4. Roll into balls and dip in toppings of your choice – sprinkles or chocolate chips, if desired. If toppings aren't sticking, wet the outside of the balls slightly with hand.

5. Store in the fridge or freezer. If in freezer, defrost a few minutes before eating.

YOGURT OAT BLUEBERRY MUFFINS

PREP TIME
15
Minutes

COOK TIME
15
Minutes

SERVINGS
12

1 cup (8 ounces) dairy-free vanilla yogurt

¼ cup plant-based milk

1 egg (replacer)

1 teaspoon vanilla

⅓ cup agave or maple syrup

1 cup old-fashioned rolled oats

¾ cup flour (gluten free, optional)

1 teaspoon baking powder

½ teaspoon baking soda

¼ teaspoon Himalayan salt

1 to 2 cups blueberries

4 tablespoons Earth Balance butter or coconut oil (melted)

1. Preheat the oven to 375 degrees. Line a 12-cup muffin tin with liners or grease with nonstick cooking spray. Set aside.

2. In a medium bowl, whisk together the yogurt, milk, egg replacer, vanilla, and agave.

3. In a large bowl, whisk together the oats, flour, baking powder, baking soda, and salt. Add the blueberries and toss to combine.

4. Add the yogurt mixture and melted butter to the dry ingredients and stir until just combined. (Don't overmix or the muffins might be dense.)

5. Portion the batter evenly among the muffin cups. Bake for 14-15 minutes until the tops spring back lightly to the touch.

6. Let the muffins cool for a few minutes in the tin and then remove them to a cooling rack to cool completely. These muffins freeze very well or keep at room temperature for a few days (well covered in Tupperware or plastic freezer bag.

Tip: You can also use plant-based chocolate chips in place of the blueberries.

CHICKPEA BROWNIES

PREP TIME
5
Minutes

COOK TIME
20
Minutes

SERVINGS
9-12

1 15-ounce can chickpeas, drained and rinsed.

½ cup nut butter (We like almond or peanut butter.)

½ cup maple syrup

1 tablespoon melted coconut oil (canola oil works as well)

1 teaspoon vanilla

¼ cup almond flour

¼ cup cocoa powder

¼ teaspoon baking soda

¼ teaspoon baking powder

¼ teaspoon Himalayan salt

½ cup chocolate chips and more for sprinkling on top (optional)

1. Preheat oven to 350 degrees.

2. In a food processor, blend chickpeas, nut butter, maple syrup, coconut oil, and vanilla.

3. Once blended, add in almond flour, cocoa powder, baking soda, baking powder, and Himalayan salt.

4. Continue to process, scraping down sides as necessary until smooth.

5. Once creamy and smooth, take off lid, remove blade, and stir in chocolate chips.

6. Do not process the chips.

7. Pour into greased 8"x8" oven safe pan and sprinkle with chocolate chips if desired.

8. Bake for 20-24 minutes.

Tip: You can add pecans, walnuts, or peanuts.

MONSTER COOKIE BARS

PREP TIME
10
Minutes

COOK TIME
15
Minutes

SERVINGS
40

½ cup Earth Balance butter, softened

1 cup packed brown sugar

1 cup granulated sugar

1½ cups creamy peanut butter

3 tablespoons egg replacer

1 tablespoon vanilla extract

1½ cup quick oats (gluten free, optional)

3 cups old-fashioned oats

1 teaspoon baking soda

1½ cup Unreal M&Ms or chocolate chips

½ cup chocolate chips (optional)

2 scoops plant-based protein powder (optional)

1. Heat oven to 350 degrees. Prepare a cookie sheet by lining with parchment paper, Silpat liner, or cooking spray.

2. In a large bowl, combine butter, brown sugar, granulated sugar, and peanut butter. Mix until fluffy and pale in color. About 1-2 minutes.

3. Make the egg replacer according to the package instructions. Add in the vanilla extract, and mix both together in large bowl.

4. Add in the oats and baking soda. Mix until combined.

5. Add in the M&Ms and chocolate chips. Stir together with a wooden spoon or spatula until combined.

6. Dump dough onto the cookie sheet and spread out. This will take several minutes, but it can be done. It helps if you dollop spoonfuls of dough all over the cookie sheet and spread it out. Sprinkle the reserved M&Ms and chocolate chips on top (if desired). Press down slightly into dough.

7. Bake for 15-17 minutes. The edges will be lightly browned, and the middle will still look pale and underdone, but it will finish baking as it cools. Let cool for at least an hour so the bars can firm up and come together. Be sure not to overbake these.

Tip: You can also use half of a banana to substitute for 1 egg in most recipes. We use this method most when baking. When making, you must mash and stir banana for 1-2 minutes.

BANANA SPLIT

PREP TIME
5
Minutes

COOK TIME
5
Minutes

SERVINGS
2

1 banana

1 scoop plant-based chocolate ice cream

1 scoop plant-based vanilla ice cream

1 scoop plant-based strawberry ice cream

2 tablespoons plant-based chocolate sauce (optional)

3 cherries

1 scoop So Delicious whipped cream

1. Slice the banana in half lengthwise and place the halves on either side of a banana split boat dish.

2. Add the scoops of ice cream between the slices of bananas. Top each scoop of ice cream with the chocolate sauce.

3. Top with whipped cream and cherries. Enjoy immediately.

Tip: You can turn this into a breakfast banana split by replacing the whipped cream and ice cream with plant-based yogurt and adding granola.

OOEY GOOEY BUTTER CAKE

PREP TIME
20
Minutes

COOK TIME
40
Minutes

SERVINGS
12-15

½ cup Earth Balance butter

4 tablespoons egg replacer

1 box yellow cake mix (check ingredients on the back to find the one with no animal products)

8 ounces plant-based cream cheese

3¾ cups powdered sugar

1. Pre-heat the oven to 350 degrees.

2. Start by melting the butter for the crust.

3. Make 2 eggs from egg replacer (instructions on the back of the package) and mix with the melted butter.

4. Mix the butter and egg replacer mixture with the cake mix.

5. Spread the mixture in an un-greased 9"x13" cake pan.

6. Mix the remaining 2 eggs from egg replacer, the cream cheese, and the powdered sugar.

7. Spread the mixture onto the crust as a second layer to the cake.

8. Bake at 350 degrees for about 40 minutes, or until a toothpick or cake tester comes out barely gooey.

9. Once the cake is fully cooked, remove it from the oven and allow it to cool for about 10–15 minutes.

10. Then using a powder shaker, sprinkle powdered sugar lightly over the entire cake (optional).

11. Allow the cake to cool completely before serving.

BAKED CINNAMON
APPLE CHIPS

PREP TIME
5
Minutes

COOK TIME
2 hrs 30
Minutes

SERVINGS
6

2 large sweet crisp apples, such as honey crisp, fuji, jazz, or pink lady.

¾ teaspoon ground cinnamon

1. Place racks in the upper and lower thirds of your oven and preheat your oven to 200 degrees. Line two baking sheets with parchment paper or a Silpat mat.

2. Wash the apples. With an apple corer or very small cookie cutter, core the apples. (You can also skip this step if you don't mind a few seeds in the chips.) With a mandolin (recommended) or a very sharp knife, slice the apples horizontally into ⅛-inch thick rounds.

3. Arrange the apples in a single layer on the prepared baking sheets. Sprinkle with cinnamon. Bake for 1 hour in the upper and lower thirds of the oven. Remove the baking sheets and switch the pans' position on the upper and lower racks. Continue baking for 1 to 1½ additional hours, until a single apple chip removed from the oven is crisp when set out at room temperature for 2 to 3 minutes. (To test the apple chips, remove a single apple slice but let the others continue baking.) Once you are happy with the crispness (the total time will vary based on the thickness of your slice and the type of apple), turn off the oven and to crisp further, let the apples sit in the oven for 1 hour as it cools down (unless you fear you overcooked them, in which case remove the pan immediately and let it sit at room temperature).

Tip: Thin slices are best. If you slice the apples more than ⅛ inch thick, they will still be delicious, but they won't be crisp. You can store apple chips in an airtight container at room temperature for up to 1 week.

PEANUT BUTTER CHOCOLATE COVERED BANANAS

PREP TIME
15
Minutes

COOK TIME
15
Minutes

SERVINGS
30

3 ripe bananas

⅓ cup natural peanut butter

½ cup semi-dark chocolate chips

2 teaspoon coconut oil (any oil will work)

1. Peel and slice bananas into rounds about ¼ inch thick.

2. Line a platter or a small baking sheet with parchment paper. Place about ½ teaspoon of peanut butter on a banana slice and top it with another banana slice to make a little banana peanut butter sandwich. Keep doing this until all banana slices are used and you have about 30 bites. Place bites on two parchment lined platters or plates, and place in the freezer to harden for about 1 hour.

3. Once banana bites have been in the freezer for over an hour, melt your chocolate by adding chocolate and coconut oil to a saucepan on medium-low heat. Stir for 2 minutes until chocolate is completely melted. This shouldn't take more than a few minutes.

4. Once chocolate is melted, remove one platter of your frozen banana bites from the freezer. Dip each frozen banana bite into the melted chocolate so that half of each bite is coated. You can coat the full bite or drizzle it with chocolate.

5. Place chocolate covered bites back on the parchment paper lined platter. Place back in freezer to harden up. Grab your second platter and continue until all the bites have been dipped. Let both platters of chocolate covered bites harden in the freezer for about 15 mins.

6. At this point, you're ready to enjoy, or you can transfer the bites into a freezer safe storage container for later. They should last for at least 1-2 months in the freezer.

Tip: When you store the banana bites for a longer period, they can get pretty hard, so you'll want to take them out of the freezer and let them thaw for 5 minutes before eating.

www.ingramcontent.com/pod-product-compliance
Lightning Source LLC
Chambersburg PA
CBHW062333150426
42813CB00079B/2869